RENEWABLE ENERGY PRINCIPLES

THE TRUTH ON THE CURRENT ENERGY CRISIS

By Anmol Brar

Sustainability Energy LLC, Publisher

This text publication is designed to provide accurate and authoritative information regarding renewable energy principles. It is sold with the understanding that the publisher is not offering legal or consulting services.

Table of Contents

The Hidden Free Energy Technology 6

Current Sources of Renewable Energy.......33

    Solar...33

    Wind...38

    Hydro Electric 43

    Biomass 48

    Geothermal 54

Current Sources of Polluting Energy 60

    Coal..68

    Natural Gas....................................71

    Nuclear Power 75

    Oil (Crude) 79

        Fuel Prices.................................87

Final Words 90

Thank you for purchasing this book and what you are about to read is some of the most important knowledge known to humankind. It's greater than the computer and its potential impact is larger than the space shuttle. However, I want to start off by giving you this disclaimer. What I am about to tell you is the truth and you may be skeptical, but it is the truth. I've spent many years researching the following topic of free energy and I've seen with my own eyes the proof that is out there. Free energy is any technology that is renewable, non-polluting, and outputs more energy than is consumed. Many people including top scientists say this is impossible, they call these perpetual motion machines yet, average people experimenting with certain types of technology have proved this is possible. If we use free energy machines to power our factories and run our cars and trucks the price of all goods would drop and the standard of living would triple.

The truth is that the rich don't want to share and want the rest of the world to live in the darkness. There's a reason why they say 80% of the wealth is held by 20% of the people. We have the technology to live a better life with all the modern conveniences but without the big expense or environmental pollution - it really is a win-win situation. This technology is being kept from the public just so a certain few people can make billions from us. It sounds sick but it's true. These people have intimidated and killed just to keep this technology out of the hands of the average person.

This book is divided into 3 main sections. The first section is about the amazing technology that will generate free energy that we currently have but is begin hidden from us. The second section is about our current types of renewable energy technologies such as solar, wind, and hydro electric. Then, the third section is about our current polluting sources of energy that we use such as coal, oil, and natural gas. I hope after reading this book you will go tell others and help fix this great problem because if not it's only going to get worse.

The Hidden Free Energy Technology

America is a grand country of over 300 million people with an unquenchable thirst for energy. We make up only 5% of the world's population but use a shocking 26% of the total world's energy supply. That's right, we use 5 times more energy on average than any other individual in the rest of the world. Way to go America! However, according to the Department of Energy, only 7% of that energy comes from renewable energy sources because 85% of the energy we use is produced from fossil fuels such as coal, oil, or natural gas and 8 percent comes from nuclear power. So how much does all this energy cost us a year? Well its about $440 billion! That $440 billion breaks out to be $200 billion paid for by residential consumers like you and me, $100 billion goes for commercial use like manufacturing then the last $140 billion goes for government buildings like hospitals, public schools, post offices, and town halls. If a veggie burger meal at your favorite restaurant costs $5 and you wanted to feed every man, woman, and child on this planet, all 6.5 billion of us could have lunch at this restaurant for almost 14 times or just about everyday for two weeks. Or, you could give every American, all 300 million of us, a check for 1447 dollars. Either way, it's a lot of money being spent on something we could get for free. I don't know about you but I'm getting sick of these high gasoline prices and what about the gas and electric companies sticking it to us every month on the energy bill. Yeah! Do these corporate fat cats think we are made of money? There's simply got to be a better solution to this problem. Well, in the president's 2006 advanced energy initiative, George W. Bush is quoted as saving 'Keeping America competitive requires reliable affordable and clean supplies of energy'. The answer is zero emission coal fired power plants, solar and wind technologies, and clean safe nuclear power. He even wanted to get us to use electric cars that run for 40 miles. Well, electric cars have come along way since then and are great, but they are no good if the energy source required to fuel them is derived from fossil fuels. Think about that. While a vehicle that runs on electricity does not directly use gasoline it does use coal and natural gas as an indirect form to supply the electricity. Well, there's no nobility in that if you ask me.

How about a car that runs off air? My buddy John sent me an email about it and after seeing that I went and did some more research. There's a French company called Motor Development International owned by Guy Negre. He invented a car that runs off compressed air. Now we've had air tools that will run on this for many years however, they are the first to power a car from it. The car is called the City and is made for short distances. It has a top speed of 68 miles an hour and can go a distance of 125 miles. It costs approximately $12,800 and it can be filled up at gas stations with the compressed air hose with a special adapter. Imagine that! You could fill up your car like you fill up a bicycle tire. You can also plug it into the wall and recharge the compressed air that way too. The company began its origins in 2000 and is still in operation today. Many concept vehicles have been released and they have also signed an exclusive agreement with Tata Motors to bring these vehicles to market. This technology simply has not gotten the attention it deserves. In 2016, it has been reported Guy Negre founder of MDI, suddenly died.

Back in 2003, in his state of the union address, President Bush announced the $1.2 Billion hydrogen fuel initiative to make reliable hydrogen powered fuel cells. Currently, hydrogen could be made from fossil fuels, nuclear power, or renewable energy. Well here's a bright idea. Do you know where else you can make hydrogen from? How about water! That's right, good old h2O. Remember, water is made from hydrogen and oxygen. In fact, 67% hydrogen and 33% oxygen. Now, you may have heard there is a lack of water on this planet, but this is not true. There is a lack of safe, potable, drinkable water. Just think for a minute about all the lakes, oceans, and seas out there. In fact, seventy percent of this planet is water so why can't we just run cars off water, well we can. There is a guy in Grove City, Ohio who did just that. His name is Stanley Meyers and he built a machine that could run your car off tap water, sea water, rainwater, or even melted snow. His dream was to help solve the world's energy problem. His device would cost $1500, convert your car to run on water, get 100 miles to the gallon, and a 40% power increase. What this means is if you have a car with a 200-horsepower motor and by just switching it to run on water it would make 80 horse power more or 280 total. Who wouldn't want something like this? Well shortly after receiving 50 million dollars from private investors to build a research and manufacturing plant Stanley Myers suddenly died. On March 21st, 1998 while eating dinner at a local Grove City Ohio restaurant he jumped out of his chair and ran to the parking lot screaming he had been poisoned. Later the autopsy report showed he had a brain aneurysm. Sounds pretty fishy to me. I mean who wouldn't want everyone to have clean renewable energy for practically nothing.

The best part about using water as a fuel source is that it becomes water again. This fuel is called HHO and there are a couple ways to make it from water. One way can be electrolysis or other is Stanley Meyers way. The electrolysis is definitely the easiest but also the least efficient. This process takes electricity and forces the water into hydrogen and oxygen. Pure water does not conduct electricity, it is the minerals in the water that actually conduct. So, to help this process along you add an electrolyte. This is usually some type of corrosive material such as salt, lye, or even citric juice. Hydrogen garage uses a base that is not corrosive, they use baking soda. With this type, you can either build your own or buy a kit. These kits only produce about 5 pounds per square inch. Now that is not enough pressure to run your car completely off of, but it does add about 50% better gas mileage. You can also get access to the plans and build it from scratch from parts from stores such as Home Depot or Lowes.

The more efficient method is to make a unit like Stanley Meyers because this process uses sound to break water and is much more effective if you want a car that gets 100 miles per gallon. There are boxes that hook up to a water cell that break it down into HHO gas with the least amount of current.

This setup is more intended to run the car on just this gas instead of the gasoline water hybrid in the example. If you do go the all water route you will need to adjust the timing, it needs to be delayed. It should fire around top, dead, center. The patents that explain Stanley Meyers process are now public domain. This means they are free for people to experiment with. The patent numbers are 4936961 and there is also a design patent 5149409. I have read people having success with the frequency of somewhere between 32 kilohertz and 42 kilohertz. But this depends on the setup of the cell. Most systems are setup with a variable frequency that can be adjusted for between 2 kilohertz to about 120 kilohertz with a square pulse.

A Japanese company called Genepax has created an engine that makes electricity from water. To show that it works, an electric car called REVAi was powered by it. There machine uses water to generate electricity and the electricity then drives the car. The REVAi sold 4600 vehicles by 2009. The model tested was a 300-watt system. The machine works by making hydrogen with a reaction between metal hydride and water. The cost of the vehicle was around $7000 USD.

The biggest problem with running cars on water is that its practically free and some people just don't like that.

Now you may be thinking great, that's cool but you can't run the world on water. Well, I'm not here today to convince you to run the world on water, no there's a much better way. A way we won't go thirsty in the process. What if we could pull free energy right out of thin air.

What I'm talking about isn't wind power or even magic this is pure electrical energy in unlimited supplies. We are surrounded by it and it's everywhere and can be tapped into simply like turning on the faucet. See the earth is a big spinning ball of iron rotating around the sun in a vast sea of electromagnetic energy and this energy can be accessed from any point in the universe.

This type of energy is called zero-point energy and it is the energy available at absolute zero. It taps into the quantum fluctuations of space and time. For example, to show how a regular electric motor is interacting with the environment around it let's look at this effect called the Aspden effect. This was named after Dr. Harold Aspden. It has been discovered that an electrical motor will take less time to start back up if the motor is turned off waiting for it to come to a complete stop then turn right back on. Let's say you have a motor that runs at 1500 rpm or revolutions per minute. When you first start the motor, it will take 20 to 30 seconds to get up to its operating speed. Now, if you turn off the motor wait for it to come back to a complete stop and then turn it back on it will only take 5 seconds for it to come up to its 1500 RPM operating speed. This effect will only last 2 or 3 minutes. After that, it will take the full time for the motor to get back up to its operating speed. So, what is happening here is that this motor is emitting a field that is somehow connecting to the active environment around the machine to pull power out of it.

Just goes to show you that there are things happening here that we cannot see and that are not explained through current electrical engineering principles and the interesting fact is that only 5% of the world around us is physical, the other 95% we can't see.

There is a man named Thomas Bearden that has a machine called MEG which stands for Motionless Electromagnetic Generator. This guy is a real Mr. wizard, he has a master's degree in nuclear engineering and was a lieutenant colonel in the US Army. After the military he worked for 17 years at several aerospace companies. His device would make 2500 Watts with no moving parts and a 10,000-watt version to follow. On average, a small home would use about 1000 to 1500 Watts an hour, so these machines have plenty of power to run your home. It worked by using 2 magnetic cores with 2 control coils and 2 output coils. As shifts occur between each core and produces more energy than what is needed to run the machine. According to Thomas Bearden, a very simple free energy project can be built with a permanent magnet and a charged capacitor. All you need to do is put this charge capacitor on top of the magnet so that the electric field is at right angles from the magnetic field of the magnet. This simple example will pull free energy right out of the environment. Now, the idea of free energy is not new and has been known for at least 100 years maybe even 150 years.

In the early 1900's Dr. T Henry Moray of Salt Lake City Utah built another free energy machine. His machine weighed 60 pounds and put out 50,000 Watts of power for free. That's enough energy to power 50 average size homes. Moray even wrote a book called the 'Sea of Energy in which the Earth Floats'. Sometimes while testing his machine for interviews, he would let some people take it apart and inspect it and then he would reassemble it and show them how it would still produce free energy. Even after countless showings, he could never get funding to manufacture his machines.

Then, in November 1933 doctor Nicolai Tesla, one of the greatest scientists of all time claims to have harnessed this cosmic energy also. You may have never heard of Tesla (besides the car), but I bet you're familiar with some of his inventions like alternating current, you know that stuff you plug your television into. Well, he had an Aerocar with an electric motor and a free energy machine. It was reported to go over eighty miles an hour, ran quiet, and never needed fuelling. The electric motor was powered by his oscillator shuttle circuit. It works by ping ponging the electricity in the circuit back and forth between two accumulators. An example of an accumulator would be a capacitor or rechargeable battery. Many circuits will use just one accumulator and destroy the magnetic effect. This effect is what pulls the free energy out of the environment. Electric cars would work great if you get rid of the heavy batteries and make electrical energy on the fly for free. Practically, you would have an electric car with unlimited batteries that would be lighter, faster, cheaper, and with unlimited energy.

During the 1930s in Russia researchers at the University of Moscow built and tested parametric oscillator generators. These work like a swing that you probably remember as a kid playing on. A few pumps of your legs at the right time then stopping and letting gravity do its part could really build up a lot of momentum. These work just like that because they supposedly outputted more energy than is needed to run them.

Back in America in the late nineteen thirties another scientist Gabriel Kron knew how to make free energy too. He was a chief scientist at General Electric. He invented an electrical circuit called a negative resistor and it would power conventional circuits just like a battery. A negative resistor gathers surrounding energy from the environment and directs it into the circuit. He was working on a network analyzer at Stanford University and stated that when the generator was turned off, it would still run because of his negative resistor. Instead of tying all circuits to a single ground a combination of open and closed circuits reportedly makes it possible.

Gabriel Kron mentored Flyod Sweet while working at GE in the 1950s. Sweet went on to build his own machine that would output 500 Watts of power from only 33 milliwatts which is 15,667 times efficient. So, theoretically you could have a machine that would run your whole house and would use less energy than a flashlight. How great would it be to never have an electricity bill every month?

His machine used special barium ferrite magnets that were conditioned to vibrate on their own to pull energy right out of the environment. This negative resistor effect was recently found in carbon fiber composites. It was discovered that a piece of carbon fiber when cured at high pressure will generate current like a battery. Now you're probably thinking that if all this is really possible why aren't there any awards? Well, how about a Nobel Peace Prize that was awarded in 1957. That's right, there was a Nobel Peace Prize awarded to Chen Ning Yang and Tsung-Dao (T.D.) Lee in December 1957. That's over 50 years ago, why haven't we harnessed this power yet? Their strong prediction of broken symmetry of opposite charges like a common bar magnet was responsible for extracting tons of energy from the active environment around us.

Proof was confirmed by Chein Shiung Wu and starting a revolution in physics in the 50's. Yet for some reason this is not mentioned in any current electrical engineering or physics book out there.

Have you ever gone out to your car in the morning to find a dead battery? Yeah, I know that really sucks. Especially when you're already running late. Well, I do have some good news for you. You never have to worry about a battery going dead in our nuclear missiles.

You know the ones that are pointed at the rest of the world in case they tick us off or won't give us their oil? We have free energy circuits powering those. Westinghouse patented these in 1966. They were in the original Minute Man missiles.

They deliberately tampered with the circuit to stop this effect and then quietly patented the process. It used a frequency converter with 64 transistor stages that would feed forward and feedback the electricity in the circuit to produce an over unity effect. These reportedly output 105 % to 115% efficiency.

In 1977 a man named Bruce Depalma invented a device called an N field generator. Bruce studied electrical engineering at Harvard in 1958 then later taught physics at MIT for 15 years. His homopolar generator produced 5 times the power than needed to run it.

A larger prototype was built called the Sunkist. It was tested at Stanford in 1986 by Dr. Robert Kincheloe. He noted that the drag on the machine was only 13-20% of a conventional generator rated at 100% efficiency. This meant that the machine could output 500% more than was input to it.

It was pulling the extra energy right out of the air that surrounded the machine. In the many years after testing this machine 200 different patents have been applied for, all being denied. It was reported that he had a 100,000-watt unit running his home. However, with this much power you could run 100 average size homes. Depalma was working on a commercial version that would have cost $500. Building on his machine, DePalma worked with an engineer, Paramahamsa Tewari. He was a senior engineer with India's Department of Atomic Energy-Nuclear Power Corporation. Tewari invented his own version of Depalma's design. It's called the Space Power Generator or SPG.

With a 5000-watt input, the SPG reportedly yielded 30,000 watts of electrical output. That's enough for three homes. Depalma's website describes both machines in more detail.

Both of these machines are based on a very old, and little-known principle of English scientist Michael Faraday. Faraday is best known for inventing the electrical motor. But it was another discovery he made, that provided a basis for free energy extraction.

On Dec 26, 1831 he discovered that space itself was magnetic. So, when spinning a magnet through it, it will create an electrical charge. This is done by using a round magnet with a copper disc cemented on top and a bolt through the center. This design increases output to more than is needed to run it.

While experimenting with these types of machines a crazy effect was produced. Now remember back to science class when they told us that gravity accelerated all objects evenly in a vacuum. That means with no wind resistance or anything. So, if you were to drop a bowling ball and a feather off a roof except for wind resistance they should fall at the same speed.

Well Depalma had this demonstration he did something called the spinning ball experiment.

He would take two identical ball bearings. Like what you find in a pinball machine. He would suspend then from the ceiling at the same height. Then he would drop them at the same time. However, before he dropped them, he would spin one of them and the one that he spun always hit the floor first. This is definitely something remarkably going on here.

The Japan Science foundation awarded two grants to local universities to study these machines. The Kazama Giken Corporation is also producing them for research. Panasonic is also looking into it.

Another company in Japan came up with a completely different way to make free energy. In 1995, Hitachi came up with a way of self-switching of the magnetic path in magnetic motors. This results in doubling a motors output. This technique used with high efficiency motors was getting an output of 1.2. – 1.6. That's 120 % to 160% efficient.

Back in America yet another inventor built a free energy device. John Bedini's machine is 800% efficient and was successfully duplicated by 26 other researchers. His motor worked by using pulsed scalar waves out of phase, to tap the energy all around us.

These waves were first discovered and published in a 1903 article by Edmund Taylor Whittaker an English mathematician. Scalar longitudinal waves come from the 4th dimension, time space. If fact, time is really condensed energy. Very similar to the energy that is in condensed in matter. Any scalar potential is really an electromagnetic energy wind.

In Northern Idaho, a 10-year-old girl built a free energy machine for her school science fair. She amazed her teachers and won first prize. It was based on an early design of John Bedini's machine. This machine used a motor, a generator, a battery and a switch.

It's cool how this works. The motor is connected to the generator with a belt. The generator is rated at 14 volts and the motor is rated at 12. This is important because you want to produce more than is required to start the motor.

The motor, generator and battery are all connected by the switch. When this run, the current first scores to the motor which remember is connected also to the generator by a belt, then when the motor is spinning, the current is turned off then the electricity generated by generator is fed back to the battery.

This concept is called back popping. It will recharge many batteries and is a simple way to generate free energy.

There is one more guy I would like to tell you about that has successfully tapped free energy. His name is John Hutchison. He is a Canadian researcher who came up with a crystal energy generator. It puts out 1.5 volts at 1 amp. So about 100 watts. This could be used to run a cell phone or laptop. Imagine never having to recharge your cell phone? How convenient would that be?

As you can see there are many ways to generate free energy. You can get it from water to rotating shafts to magnets to even crystals. All these machines are somehow making a simple dipole that is extracting the free energy out of the atmosphere.

A simple dipole can be a battery, the terminals of a generator, any two-pole magnet like a bar magnet. An atom with positive and negative charges, the earth's magnetic field, the sun, or even another galaxy.

Current electrical systems deliberately only use their current once and do not replenish it from the active environment. All electrical circuits have been deliberately forced into being equal with the active environment around it.

With this setup, circuits are made to consume the energy instead of replenishing it. It's too bad considering if the circuit was tuned to be out of balance it would make more energy than we could ever use.

The truth is, there is tons of energy all around us to use! We are literally floating in vast sea of free energy. The choice really comes down to will we use it. The only reason we are currently using the same old sources is purely greed.

The giant energy companies make 440 billion dollars a year from us for something we could get for practically nothing. How sick is that!

Just think about it for a minute. How much do you spend a month on energy? You know things like gasoline, gas to heat your home and electricity to run all your stuff. 200 a month, 400, 600?

Imagine having that extra money in your pocket every month. Well 400 a month in savings adds up to almost 5000 a year. Imagine what else you could do with that money? You could save it for college or take a vacation.

So, tell your friends, family and co workers. And the next time you hear somebody complaining about rising gas prices or out of control heating bills tell them about this technology.

Current Sources of Renewable Energy

In this chapter, I want to talk about our current sources of renewable energy. They're getting better but not at all as efficient as a technology we could be using. It's like an old 1909 Ford Model T trying to race a brand-new red Ferrari, it just can't compete.

Solar

When you think about renewable energy, solar power is usually one of the first ones that come to mind. We receive enough energy from the sun in one day to power the world for 27 years. If plants can do it why can't we? It takes about 8 minutes and 20 seconds for the sun's energy to reach the earth. One of the first uses of the sun for energy was in 1830 by British astronomer John Herschel. He had a box used to absorb sunlight to collect heat and cook food while on an expedition in Africa. Then in 1954 photovoltaic cells were discovered by Bell Telephone that converted sunlight into electricity. These are used in late 1950s to power US space satellites. A solar cell is a non mechanical device made of silicone alloys and when you have a bunch of solar cells, they make up a solar panel. When you have a bunch of solar panels, they make up a solar array and all these solar cells are just hanging out in the sun collecting energy. Sunlight is made of photons and when these photons strike the solar cells some of them are absorbed. The electrons are freed from the photons and generate direct current like a battery. In areas that receive good yearly sunshine, solar panels can be put up on your roof and they can be designed to power some or all of your electrical needs. Well how about a solar powered car? Ventura, a French car company made a car that runs completely on solar power it's a 4-person city car that goes

32 miles an hour with a distance of 31 miles. It weighs about 722 pounds and is powered by a 22-horsepower electric motor. It gets its charge from a 2 foot by 4-foot area of solar cells on the roof which is about 8 square feet and really looks more like a golf cart, but it shows you what is possible. Now if you're interested in a solar powered speedster that goes faster than 32 miles an hour checkout the University of Michigan solar racing team. They are one of the most successful solar race teams in North America. They won the North American solar challenge 4 times. Their car weighs about 800 pounds, holds two people and goes 75 miles an hour. It's powered though by 5000 solar cells in an area about 5 feet by 7 feet which is about 35 square feet. The greatest thing about solar power is it after you purchase and install the equipment the energy that it produces is free plus it doesn't pollute when it's making this power. Solar power can be used in just about any location,

but the output would depend on how much sunlight you received. Also, there are very little moving parts if any to wear out and you could even get financial incentives to help pay for systems. A major disadvantage to solar energy is the upfront cost because it can be expensive to purchase the equipment, and have it installed plus you can't use solar power at night or in bad weather. The output is very dependant on how much sunlight you get so this can be great in California but bad in Chicago.

Solar panels also take up a lot of space and your roof may not be at the correct angle to capture the sun. Currently, solar panels are only 30% efficient and then degrade and breakdown overtime. California a state with lots of sunshine it trying to cash in on it. Southern California Edison is building a massive solar installation. It will cover two square miles of roof tops with solar cells and power 162,000 homes. It is about 250 mega watts of power. Half as much power as a coal or natural gas power plant would produce. California's goal was to get 20% of its energy use from solar by 2010. To help this along. Govern Arnold Schwarzenegger wanted to pass a bill that would help to pay for the cost of these setups. As of 2016, only ten percent of the total electricity production comes from solar power.

A similar plan in Japan, helped drop the cost by 50 % over 10 years. Japan is currently the largest market for solar products. The average home uses about 1 kilowatt or 1000 watts per hour. With 730 hours per month you get about 10 watts per square foot, so for every 1000 watts we need about 100 square feet. If we got sunlight 24 hours a day then all we would need is 100 sq. feet. However, we don't so we need 400 to 800 square feet. This would cost about $35, 000 to $50,000 and would pay back in 20 years. The goal would be to cut this cost in half and payback in ten years. These numbers are based on today's price for electricity. If the price increases the payback would be sooner.

Wind

Wind energy is the fastest growing energy source in the world. The US ranks third in the world in wind power capacity behind Germany and Spain. In the 1920's wind power was a significant source of energy for rural America. Wind machines in the US generate about 17 billion kilowatt hours of electricity per year. That's enough to power a city the size of Chicago.

There are two types of windmills, vertical and horizontal. The first wind mills were vertical axis systems developed in Persia about 500 to 900 AD. They were used to pump water and grind grain.

Vertical axis windmills were also used in China. The first documented one was in 1219 AD. They used reeds to make sails to catch the wind. They were also used to pump water and grind grain. These first vertical axis windmills did not work so well. Half of the sail area had to be covered to get the other side to spin.

Then in the 1300's in Holland the first horizontal wind mills appeared. These worked much better because all the sails were used to catch the wind instead of half with the others. They used sails like a sail boat to catch the wind. Then in the 1800's the wind mill grew in popularity with the expansion of the American west.

They were made from metal and used to pump water. Between 1850 and 1870 there were over 6 million small 1 horse power or less windmills in use. Larger ones were used to pump water for steam railroad trains.

The first use of a large windmill to generate electricity was in 1888. A man named Charles Brush from Cleveland Ohio. His machine used a picket fence type of rotor 55 feet in diameter. It was the first windmill to use a gearbox to step up the speed to drive a direct current generator.

Windmills work by using aerodynamic lift. This is the same force that makes an airplane fly. The passing wind turns the rotor which turns a shaft that can be harnessed to do work. Such as turn a generator or pump water or grind grain. In modern wind mills it turns a generator to produce electricity.

A great example of wind power is the Big Spring Wind Project in Texas. It has 46 wind turbines that generate enough electricity to power 7,300 homes. Southern California Edison is building a 50 square mile wind farm. This is 3 times larger than any current wind farm. It will generate about 1,500 megawatts and power almost a million homes.

The advantages of wind power are many. First off it is fueled by the wind. It is a clean energy source it doesn't pollute. It is a local domestic source of energy and our wind supple is very abundant. Wind mills also use a small foot print of land. So, in rural area when built on farms or ranches, the land can still be worked.

Wind energy is actually a type of solar energy. It is caused by the heating of the atmosphere by the sun, the rotating of the earth, and the earth's surface irregularities.

The disadvantages of wind are these. Wind must compete with other conventional forms of energy on a cost basis and may not be the cheapest. Even though the cost of wind power has decreased dramatically over the last ten years; the technology requires a higher initial investment than a fossil fuel plant.

The major challenge to wind is that it is not always blowing when we need electricity and the output depends on wind speed. Also, good winds are usually out in remote areas. Far away from the cities that need the electricity. Wind plants can also be noisy, but much less than a fossil fuel plant. Currently windmills are only 30 - 40 % efficient.

Wind technology has come a long way. It is starting to mature and be commercialized. World wide there are about 10 – 12 manufactures of large utility scale systems making 200 kilowatts to 3.2 megawatt systems. There are also several companies building small windmills making 1000 watts up to 10,000 watts. These are more suited for personal use.

There is a great product made
by WindSide that has been dubbed the urban
wind mill. It produces about 1100 watts. It is
3.5 feet wide and 12 feet tall and weighs 2000
pounds These cost about $12,000 dollars.

A far better way to generate energy is with
magnets. This type of technology can be over
100% efficient and still works when the wind
is not blowing. This technology is real and
being suppressed. Visit energybook.info for
more information.

Hydro Electric

Hydro electric power is the most widely used
form of renewable energy. According to
Wikipedia, it supplies 19% of the world's
energy. Brazil gets 80 percent of all their
electricity from it. The United States currently
ranks 4th in hydro electric output. China is
number one, then Canada, then Brazil then us.

7 percent of renewable energy comes from hydro.

It was first used by the Greeks to turn water wheels for grinding wheat into flour more than 2000 years ago. In 1880 Michigan's Grand Rapids Electric Light and Power Company generated electricity with a dynamo belted to a water turbine at the Wolverine chair factory. It lit up 16 brush arc lamps. Then in 1881 Niagara Falls city street lamps were powered like this too.

By 1920 25% of the US electrical generation was by hydroelectric. By 1940's 40% was generated. Unfortunately, today only 7% of our electricity comes from hydro electric according to the Department of energy.

Hydro electric power converts flowing water to electricity. Most hydro electric plants rely on a dam that holds back water to create a large reservoir or lake. Gates on the dam open and gravity pulls the water down a pipeline that builds pressure to turn a turbine. This turbine is connected by a shaft to a generator than produces electricity.

An example of a hydro electric plant is the Hoover Dam. It is located 30 miles south east of Las Vegas. It was completed in 1935 and cost 49 million dollars. The output of this Dam is 2,080 mega watts which is enough for 2 million homes.

The advantages of hydro electric are these. It is the most efficient renewable energy we currently use. It can be up to 90% efficient. Plus, the water is not destroyed by passing through the dam. They also produce inexpensive and clean power. Dams can also store rain water or water directly. Then in case of a drought, the dam will have a consistent supply of water.

Dams are a simple concept to build with low technology. This makes for very few break downs. A simple design also makes for inexpensive repairs and low maintenance costs. If needed, hydro electric plants can be turned off instantly, where fossil fuel plants take hours and nuclear plants take days.

The downside of hydro power is this. For good power production it requires flooding of entire valleys and scenic areas. It also disrupts the natural seasonal change in the river and the ecosystem can be destroyed. Rivers clog because the silt is blocked from running down to the beaches. During a drought hydro electric plants may become useless or produce much less power than planned.

If a dam ever breaks it produces a huge flash flood. There can be large amount of green house gases produced from the decaying plants after flooding an area. It also creates a large reservoir that destroys the local community already by the river. Dams are more of a large-scale project. They do not work well for individuals to power your home or business.

Hydro electric power can be a great thing. It produces lots of cheap clean renewable energy. However, in the US it has hit some snags. The amount of green house gases created from flooding can be more than a fossil fuels power plant. In the last few years it has been difficult to build large scale projects. Environmentalists and the local people living where a dam could be built have fought hard to keep them down. The focus has been on smaller dams that produce electricity for local small communities instead of massive dams that could power a whole state.

This technology is limited to needing at least 10 feet of height to generate enough pressure to make electricity. These systems might only produce 400 to 700 watts at a cost of $2500 – $8000. This can be difficult to set up if you do not have the right conditions. There is no way to set this up if you do not have a river or creek running though your back yard.

Biomass

Biomass energy is one of the oldest fuel sources around. We have burned wood for a very long time. However, today we have much more efficient ways to extract the energy.

Biomass is stored solar energy that man can convert to electricity, fuel or heat. Through photosynthesis the energy from the sun is stored in the chemical bonds of the plant material. Most biomass comes from three sources.

The first source is agriculture crop left over such as corn husks or sugar cane stalks. The second source is municipal and industrial waste. And third is from energy plantations. These are farms that grow crops for energy production. Biomass produces 3 percent of our total renewable energy.

What is biomass? Biomass is all plant materials or vegetation. It can be wild or cultivated processed or raw. Prior to the industrial revolution, biomass was used for all our energy needs. Up until the 1880's American used wood for 91% of all its energy requirements. It was used for heating and cooking in most homes. It was also used for steam in boats, trains, and manufacturing.

Then, in 1890 coal replaced wood for heating. By the 1930's half of all Americans lives in building heated with coal, but by the 1950's coal was replaced by electricity and natural gas for heating and lighting. It wasn't until the 1970's with higher energy costs did wood and corn become cheaper alternatives.

In 1984 in Burlington, VT built a 50 megawatts wood fired plant to make electricity. That's enough electricity to power 50,000 average homes. The plant was one of many built that year. 1989 pilot trials of direct wood fired gas turbine plants were conducted for the first time in the US and Canada. By the late 1990's there were 190 biomass fired electricity generating facilities outputting 6 gigawatts. That enough to power 6 million homes.

Here is how biomass works. For the longest time, the easiest way to convert the energy was to burn it. The heat is used directly for heating, cooking, and industrial uses or indirectly to make electricity.

The biggest problem with burning is that most of the energy is wasted. Today we have better ways to release the energy. Biomass can be converted into a variety of gaseous, liquid, or solid fuels. These produced can be further refined into alcohol or methane. Some sewage treatment plants and land fills can capture the methane gas coming off and produce electricity. Currently, here are the three best ways.

First up is thermal chemical. This is when plant material is heated but not burned, it breaks down into various gases liquids and solid fuels. Bio-chemical, bacteria, yeasts, and enzymes break down the carbohydrates. Then they are fermented into alcohol. When bacteria break down biomass, methane, and carbon dioxide are produced. This can be captured in a landfill or sewage treatment plants.

Second is chemical. Biomass oils like soybean and canola oil can be chemically converted into a liquid fuel like diesel fuel. Cooking oil from restaurants can be also used to make bio-diesel for trucks.

The third way is micro algae. It can be farmed to produce bio-diesel. New methods have also figured out how to make a jet fuel like kerosene. Micro algae can produce 30 – 100 times more oil than soybeans on a similar area.

The US Department of Energy estimated that if algae replaced all the petroleum fuel in the US it would take 15,000 square miles which is slightly larger than the state of Maryland. However, this is only 1/7 of the area of all the corn harvested in the United States

Some examples of biomass are fast growing trees and shrubs, agricultural residues like used vegetable oil, wheat straw, or corn. Wood waste like paper trash, yard clippings, saw dust or wood chips can be used also. Methane can be also captured from land fills and municipal waste treatment facilities.

The advantages of biomass are these. It recycles animal, food processing, and municipal wastes and it reduced the use of landfills. It also creates jobs in rural areas. Plus, growing crops help to reduce green house gases by producing oxygen.

However, the drawbacks to biomass are these. If you are using food type plants for fuel, it drives up the price of food. Plus, more green house gases are produced if you burn it. The collecting, harvesting, and storage of raw biomass materials is expensive and large volumes are needed compared to fossil fuels. It is also not as ready to use as other fuels. Some must be chipped or shredded.

Even though biomass energy does have some unique possibilities. There are much easier ways to do it.

Geothermal

Geothermal power uses heat in the earth. This heat is used to make steam to generate electricity. According to Wikipedia as of 2007 geothermal power supplied only 1% of the world energy needs. It is used commercially in over 70 countries. California has 33 plants and produces 90% of the US geothermal power. Nevada has 15, Hawaii and Utah each have one.

The direct use of hot water as an energy source goes way back to ancient times. The Roman, Chinese, and Native Americans used hot mineral springs for cooking, heating and bathing. After bathing the next most common use of geothermal power is direct use for heating. Hot water around the area can be pumped directly into buildings for heat. 95% of all heating in Reykjavik, Iceland is like this.

In 1892 Boise Idaho, first district heating started. It grew to supply 200 homes and 40 downtown businesses. Then in 1904 Prince Piero Ginori Conti invented the first geothermal electric power plant. He used a piston engine feed with steam. The steam was made from a heat exchanger filled with hot water from the well. The engine was hooked up to a 10,000-watt generator.

In 1913 after several years of safe operation, a larger 250-kilowatt geothermal power plant was built. This provided plenty of electrical power to supply all the chemical manufacturers and villages in the area. It is still in operation today. That size would power about 250 homes.

The first geothermal power plant to open in the US was in 1960. This was in Sonoma CA. The first one produced 11 megawatts of power. This area has grown to over 1000 megawatts of geothermal power. That's enough to power about 1 million homes.

Geothermal power is generated in the earth's core. 4000 miles below the surface the temperature is hotter than the surface of the sun. People use geothermal power for heat and to generate electricity. How far you must drill is dependent to how hot the water is at what depth.

There are 3 basic ways to generate electricity with geothermal power. The first is Dry Steam. This uses steam right from the geothermal reservoir to turn turbines. The second type is called Flash Steam. This method takes high pressure hot water from deep in the earth and converts it to steam to turn turbines that generate electricity.

When the water cools down and condenses back to water. It is pumped back into the ground to be used repeatedly. Most plants work like this. Temperatures for this are usually around 300-degree Fahrenheit with some newer technology that works down to 260 degrees.

The third way is called a Binary Popper plant. These transfer heat from one liquid to another. Geothermal hot water is used to turn another liquid to steam and turn a generator.

The advantages of geothermal power are these. The energy harnesses are clean and safe for the surrounding environment. It is sustainable, because the water used as steam is pumped back into the ground and used for steam again.

It is not affected by bad weather. They work day and night, 24 hours a day 365 days a year. They also work very well for base load power, with a 98% operating time. It is also very scalable. A large geothermal plant could power a city, or a smaller one could power a village. Small heat pumps for $28,000 can be a very cost-effective way to heat homes.

However, the disadvantages of geothermal power are these. Generating electricity from this can be expensive. In Germany a new 3.5-megawatt plant that's enough to power 3500 homes, cost around 47 million to 63 million. The cost of drilling a well is 60% plus this technology is not available in all locations. It is only about 35 – 40 percent efficient with a 30-year lifecycle. Geothermal power is very popular in Germany. They are building plants as fast as they can drill. In fact, they have started increasing production on well drill bits so they can drill more. Idaho also just completed one.

It produces 9 mega watts, enough to power for 2,900 homes. It is the first plant in the state. If all goes well, they want to increase output to 36 megawatts and then maybe 90 mega watts. That's enough for 90,000 homes.

Geothermal power is a great solution in certain areas of the world that can use it. However, for most of the world it is just not possible.

Current Sources of Polluting Energy

Electric Energy. What is it? Well electricity is all around us. It occurs naturally as lightning and static electricity. Its just that producing it can be tricky. It is currently a secondary source. This means that another fuel is consumed to produce it.

According to the Department of Energy, As of 2018

- 49% of the electricity we use comes from coal fired plants.
- 20% of it comes from Natural gas fired plants
- 19% comes from Nuclear power
- 7% comes Hydro electric and
- 2% comes from gasoline fired plants.
- Less than 1% comes from Solar, Wind, Biomass or Geothermal.

Except for hydro electric which is 90% efficient, most ways to generate it are at best 40% efficient. If we generated it with magnets, we would be generating electricity directly as a primary source. We are using magnetism to pull electricity right out of thin air and can achieve efficiencies greater than 100%. With many types being over 500 to 1000 % efficient.

Well let discuss the history of electricity. Where did it come from? As the story goes in 900 BC a Greek shepherd named Magnus was walking across a field with some strange magnetic rocks. These rocks ended up pulling the iron spikes out of his sandals.

Today this area is known as the Magnesia region in Greece. Then in 600BC Thales of Milton in Modern day Turkey rubs cat fur and a piece of amber together. It attracts a bird feather to stick to it.

Then in 1269 Petrus Peregrinus of Picardy, Italy discovers that natural magnets called loadstones will align a needle along the longitude lines of the earth. In 1600 an English Scientist and Court Physical to Queen Elizabeth, William Gilbert discovers that the earth is a giant magnet, just like the little loadstones.

He also coined the term electricity from the Greek word for amber. He wrote a book called De Magnete which was very influential throughout Europe. He is considered the father of electricity.

In 1752 Benjamin Franklin proved that lightning and a spark from amber were the same. He was flying a kite with an iron nail on one end and an iron key at the other end. They were tied together with some string. When lighting flashed, a tiny bit struck the nail and ran down the string to the key.

Please don't try this at home. Ben was very lucky he was not electrocuted. In 1793 Aless Andro Volta makes the first battery. Then 1819 Hans Christian Orsted discovers a magnetic field surrounds a wire when current is flowing through it.

Michael Faraday wondered if electricity could make magnetism, why can't magnetism produce electricity. Well in 1831 he found his answer. A moving magnet will produce electricity in a wire.

In 1873 James Clark Maxwell publishes his model of the electro magnetic field. These equations are the basis for modern day electrical engineering.

1879, Thomas Edison invents the light bulb. To supply electricity to those first bulbs Thomas Edison set up the Pearl street station in Lower Manhattan. On Sept 2, 1882 it started with one coal fired DC generator to power 400 light bulbs. This system grows quickly, to 6 generators to power 7,200 lights.

Then in 1888 Nikola Tesla invents the first AC motor and polyphase transmission system. This system would transmit power much farther than DC current and at higher voltages than 110v. In 1893 Westinghouse and Tesla were chosen to transmit power from Niagara Falls to the city of Buffalo NY.

The same year, they also demonstrated Tesla's Alternating current electrical system at the Chicago worlds fair. All the lighting for the whole fair was powered by this system. Shortly after our modern day 60 cycle AC system was introduced.

This is the system we use today. In the end it was Tesla's better Alternating current system that won out over Thomas Edison's Direct current system. Yet for some reason there is very little in our history books about Nikola Tesla.

In 1920's The Connecticut Valley Power exchange started to connect all the local utilities together. This helped to create our modern-day energy grid that we have. We use this to distribute power throughout the country. Electricity has been generating since 1881. The first power plants ran off flowing water or burning coal.

Currently most of our electrical generation is done through heat engines. These are engines that burn something to produce heat. This heat boils water to produce steam, and then this steam flows through a turbine to spin a generator that produces electricity. Its too bad we don't use magnets.

We could make energy greater than 100% efficiency with no pollution.

There are two types of electricity both with a positive or negative charge. They are Alternating current, and Direct Current. Some examples of AC current are the wall sockets you have in your home. Where as the DC current is like a battery such as a cell phone or regular double AA battery.

The difference between Alternating current and Direct current is this. AC current flows back and forth with the voltage going from positive and negative 60 times a second. Therefore, it called Alternating current.

It is alternating between two points 60 times a second. Where Direct current, is only flowing in one direction. It takes about 750 watts of either type to equal one horse power.

The advantages of electricity are these. It is a clean, cheap, safe and convenient source of energy. So much of our stuff runs on it too. From cell phones, to our homes, to computers, toasters, radios, you name. Electricity can also be used to start a human heart.

However, the drawbacks are this. It can shock or kill you if you are not careful. Currently most of it is produced by burning something or nuclear power. It is also expensive to use as heat.

I think the best thing for electricity would be a shift from large scale electricity generation, to more personal powered systems. You could have a small machine that runs your whole house for free. Then you could have smaller devices that can run your cell phones, computers and other toys. Once you purchase these devices, they would produce all the power you would need for free. What a great idea!

Coal

Coal energy is used to generate half of all our electricity. Coal is an old and dirty fuel. It was used as fuel to power the industrial revolution. It was also used for transportation to the west from the 1800's until the 1950's.

Coal energy has a long history. Some historians believe that coal energy was first used in China to smelt copper for weapons and coins. 1748 The first US commercial coal production began near Richmond Virginia.

In 1769, James Watt patented the modern-day steam engine. Coal energy was used to make steam for early steams engines. By the 1800's coal energy was the primary fuel used by steam powered trains.

In 1882 the first practical coal energy fired electric generation plant went in business and was supplying electricity to New York for its house hold lights. By the 1950's most industry used coal energy and most homes were heated by it.

Coal is a sedimentary organic rock that contains 40 – 90 % carbon by weight. It is formed by ancient plants and animals accumulating in moist peat bogs. As plants die off in a wet area, they pile up in to peat moss. It takes about 4,000 years to 10, 000 for 3 feet (1 meter) of peat moss to accumulate. This process works best in a river delta or coastal plains.

Over time these peat mosses are compressed by further deposits and the carbon content of the coal is concentrated. The older the coal gets the harder and blacker it is. Coal is mined to get it out of the ground. Then it is burnt to produce electricity. In the most common type of coal plants, pulverized coal is blown into a furnace, where it burns while it is airborne.

Water flows through pipes in the furnace. The water is heated to boiling and creates steam under pressure. Then this pressurized steam flows over a turbine connected to a generator to produce electricity. After the steam passed through the turbine it is cooled down into water to pass through the furnace again.

The advantages of coal energy are this. We have about 300 years of it left, but only 100 years if we used it to replace oil and gas. Coal energy is plentiful and cheap. It provides a warmer heat than electricity. The biggest advantage is that it is more abundant than oil or gas. The US has 27% of the world supply. Russia has 17%, China 12% and India 10%.

However, the disadvantages of coal energy are these. Most coal fired electric plants are only 35% efficient. Coal is very dirty to burn. It is the leading cause of green house gases. Acid rain is also caused from sulfur emissions which are produced when burning it. Plus, coal energy is not a renewable source eventually we will run out.

Natural Gas

Natural gas energy is the second largest way the Unites States generates electricity. 20% of their electricity comes from it. Also 62% of Americans use natural gas energy in stoves, furnaces, water heaters and clothes dryers. It is also a raw material used in the manufacturing of paint, fertilizer, steel, glass, paper, and clothing.

In 200 BC the Chinese used natural gas energy to make salt from salt water in gas fired furnaces. Then in 1626 French explorers discovered Native Americans burning the gases that were seeping around Lake Eire.

In 1821 in Fredonia New York, William Hart dug a 27 foot well to bring natural gas to the surface. The Fredonia Gas Company was later formed to sell this to the surrounding area. This was Americans first Natural Gas Energy Company. Then in 1859 when Edwin Drake drilled his well looking for oil, natural gas energy was also found. A two-inch pipe was run from the well 5.5 miles to the town of Titusville, Pennsylvania.

In 1885 Robert Bunsen invents the Bunsen Burner. The Bunsen Burner combined the perfect amount of air and natural gas. It created a stable flame that was used for heating and cooking. In 1891 electricity began to replace natural gas energy used for lighting. Then in 1937 natural gas energy distributors started adding Mercaptan to the gas. This is what gives natural gas the rotten egg smell.

From 1940 through the 60's the natural gas pipelines were expanded greatly. This really helped to supply the growing market. From the early 1900's to 1970's natural gas energy use had grown by 50 %.

Natural gas energy is formed like oil. Sediment gets built up, starts composing and then get squeezed into coal, oil, or natural gas. Once a natural gas mine is tapped, the natural gas energy is processed to remove other gases such as propane, butane, or carbon dioxide.

These will be saved and used as other products. Once the natural gas is cleaned and filtered it will be pumped into our homes for use. Natural gas energy is mostly a mixture of methane, ethane, and propane. Methane makes up about 73 to 95% Natural gas is usually found when looking for oil. It was once considered a hassle. It would be burnt off at the well head until oil started flowing.

The advantages of natural gas energy are these. It is the cleanest burning fossil fuel. The blue flame that you see when you burn it is almost perfect and complete combustion. This means there is little smoke, soot or odor when burning. Natural gas energy is also non toxic. It is very convenient with it being piped into your home.

You don't have to refuel like a car. We have abundant domestic sources of it. It is a dependable fuel. The pipelines are not disrupted by bad weather. About 87% of the natural gas used is produced here in the United States. Natural gas produces 60-90 % less smoke than gasoline.

However, the disadvantages of natural gas energy are these. It's still a fossil fuel and not a renewable source. It is a gas so it can be hard to capture and it's less ready to use than gasoline. Plus, natural gas energy fired plants are only 45% efficient.

Nuclear Power

Nuclear power in not a renewable energy source. They produce radioactive waste and gases. Both pose major health risks. Currently the US gets about 19 % of its electrical power from it. However, France gets about 77% of its power from it. Do you know how nuclear power came to be? Well it all started on December 2, 1942.

The first self sustaining nuclear chain reaction was completed by Enrico Fremi at the University of Chicago. It last 28 minutes and was called the Chicago Pile 1. On July 16, 1945 the first bomb was tested in

Alamogordo, New Mexico under the code name Manhattan project.

September 1945 two bombs created using this technology were dropped on Japan ending World War 2. After seeing the horrible destruction from this, in 1946 the Atomic Energy Act was passed. It stated that Nuclear energy could only be used for peaceful purposes.

In 1951 December 20th in Arco Idaho, the Experimental Breeder reactor 1 produces the first electrical power from nuclear energy lighting 4 light bulbs. Then in 1957 the worlds first large-scale nuclear power plant begins operation in shipping Port of Pennsylvania to supply electricity to the Pittsburgh area.

In 1961 the world's largest ship was built. It is the USS Enterprise nuclear powered aircraft carrier. It will reach speeds of 30 knots and has a range of 400,000 miles before refueling. All seams promising for nuclear power until March 28th, 1979.

The worst accident in US history 3-mile island near Harrisburg Pennsylvania. It was caused by a loss of coolant from the reactor cores due to mechanical malfunction and human error. No one was injured and no over exposure to radiation occurred.

Then on April 26, 1986, operator error causes an explosion at the Chernobyl nuclear power plant in the former Soviet Union. The reactor had an inadequate containment building, and large amounts of radiation escaped.

Chernobyl had 50 tons of radio active material explode into the air. It covered 140,000 square miles. It was 200 times the amount of radioactive material that what was dropped on Japan in both bombs combined.

So how does a nuclear reactor work? Well at first glance nuclear power looks very simple. The broad concept is that you heat water to make steam, and then the steam propels turbines to make electricity. If you take a closer look at how this heat is produced, the topic gets a bit more complicated.

With a fossil fuel plant, the fuel is burnt to produce heat. With a nuclear plant you have two ways to produce heat, Nuclear Fusion and Fission. With Fusion energy is released when atoms are combined or fused together to form a larger atom. This is how the sun works.

Nuclear fission splits atoms away to form smaller atoms and release energy. Nuclear power plants use this type to produce heat. The fuel source in Uranium. It is a scarce resource. The supply is estimated to be only around 30 –60 years depending on actual demand.

Radio active waste is extremely dangerous and can last up to 10,000 years. There is a huge risk with nuclear power, no matter how safe you build them. The consequence of an accident would be devastating. The more plants that are built, the greater chance of an accident.

As you can see nuclear power is not a great option to power our ever-increasing power demands.

Oil (Crude)

Crude oil is a dirty and polluting fuel source. According to the Energy Information Administration

69% of all the crude oil we use is for transportation. Refiners can only produce 20 gallons of gas from every 42-gallon barrel of crude oil. The rest of the barrel gets turned into other products like diesel fuel, heating oil, jet fuel, and propane. Americans use about 385 million gallons of gasoline every day. Only 50% is produced domestically, the rest is imported from other countries.

The crude oil industry began in American on August 27, 1859 when Edwin L Drake drilled 69 1/ 2 half feet well and hit oil near Titusville PA. However crude oil use goes back much farther. In 3000 BC, Mesopotamians used rock oil for architectural adhesives, ship caulks, medicines, and roads.

Then in 2000 BC, the Chinese refined crude oil for use in lamps and in heating homes.

In 1264 Marco Polo visited the Persian city of Baku and saw crude oil being collected from seeps on the ground. Moving from seeps on the surface to shallow pits and then to hand dug holes up to 115 feet deep in 1594. This could be considered the first crude oil well.

Up until the 1800's most light came from animal fat such as whale oil because it burned with less odor and smoke was very popular. This whale oil was made from the oil in the nose of a sperm whale. It was very expensive at about 2 dollars per gallon.

In today's dollars this would cost over 200 dollars a gallon. In 1856 the Unites States at the height of the industry made 4 to 5 million gallons and 6 to 10 million gallons of train oil. In 1857 a clean burning kerosene lamp was invented by Michael Dietz. With this invention pretty much over night the old whale oil burning lamps fell in popularity. The new and much cheaper kerosene lamps took over as the main source of light.

Raw crude oil and its products were used pretty much just for lamps and burning in steam powered equipment. Then in 1879 when Thomas Edison invented the light bulb this eliminated the need for kerosene. The crude oil industry went into a recession. When kerosene was distilled from crude oil, all the other products that came from it were just thrown out.

Then in 1888 when Karl Benz invented the first car the crude oil industry had a new use. In 1893 the first American car was invented by Frank and Charles Duryea. It also ran gasoline. By the 1920's American had over 9 million cars on the road.

Compare this to over 125 million now. That is a lot of cars. By the 1950's crude oil had become our most used fuel. In 1960's OPEC was formed by Iran, Iraq, Kuwait, Saudi Arabia, and Venezuela. The group has grown to 11 countries total now.

In 1973 the United States had the first oil embargo. Several countries in OPEC stopped selling crude oil to the US because of our support for Israel in the Israel Arab war. OPEC cut production by 25 %. This caused temporally shortages and tripled the price. Some gas stations ran out of fuel, while other had long lines of people waiting.

Then in 1978 – 80 crude oil prices doubled due to the Iranian Revolution. This caused 3.9 million barrels a day shortage. The other counties in OPEC eventually increased production to help.

Then in 1981 it happened again and prices double yet another time. This really goes to show you how vulnerable we are to other countries drama when we rely on them to power our lives.

The high prices caused less oil to be consumed and crude oil production began to slow. OPEC didn't like that. So, in 1986 Saudi Arabia stopped holding back production and flooded the market with cheap oil. The excess flow of crude oil caused the price to be cut in half.

Through out the late 80's and early 90's oil consumption quickly grew due to the cheap price. Today after so many years of cheap oil, it is coming back to bite us. The price has hit record levels. We need to use a better energy source than this.

What it is oil? Well crude oil is an oily, flammable liquid that is found in nature. Usually underground, but sometimes it seeps up to the surface. Over millions of years, plant and animal remains fall to the bottom of shallow bodies of water. As the water recedes the remains are covered with dirt and sediment layers. It can be clay, silt or other plant material. With the lack of oxygen this material partially decomposes and forms crude oil.

There are several products in a barrel of crude oil. Each product is refined and evaporates at a different temperature. This is how it works. Crude oil is heated, and the vapors are sorted with a distillation column. This helps to separate the gases by vapor temperature.

The first product to burn off are gases used for cooking, heating and plastics. Next is Naphtha or Ligroin. This is like gasoline and will later be converted back into it. Next is gasoline. Then Kerosene. Then Diesel fuel. Next is lubricating oil, then fuel oil, then finally tar and asphalt. This process goes from lightest to heaviest sorted by temperature.

As you can see there are many products in a barrel of crude oil. This process ranges in temperate from 68 degrees Fahrenheit for cooking gas to 158 degrees F for gasoline to 392 degrees F for diesel fuel all the way up to 1112-degree F for tar. We use these products to make so much of our stuff from fuels to roads to plastic goods.

The advantages of crude oil are these. It was readily available. It is convenient energy source to run cars on. Gasoline is easy to transport. It has been cheap for so long. Plus it was way cheaper than whale oil.

However today the disadvantage of crude oil far out way the advantages. Smoke, pollution, and green house gases are created from burning it. There is a limited amount and we are running out. We rely on foreign sources for our needs. Usually war is used to secure our interests. Just like what we are doing now

in Iraq. Plus, the price of crude oil keeps
rising and it's getting expensive.

Fuel Prices

Fuel prices are something that hits home for
every American. We are a country that is built
on the automobile. It's how we get to work
and pick up the kids from little league
practice. Unfortunately, in America our mass
transit system is under developed. So, when
fuel prices start rising, it really cuts into our
budgets. At a certain price we will complain
and take notice, but when it drops again, we
quickly forget. You would think we would
have learned a lesson or two after the first oil
crisis in 1973. Yet, today we find our selves in
a similar problem.

Just to put things into perspective. America
has over 125 million cars on the road and we
use about 400 million gallons of gasoline per

day. So, you might be wondering what can be done about this? Well we do have options, but you must be willing to have an open mind and think outside the box. Let me explain. Water is made up of hydrogen and oxygen. Both are flammable. The great thing about using water as a fuel is that when you break it down and burn it, when it cools it condenses back into water. So technically you could run the exhaust back into the fuel tank and make it a closed loop system. Plus, you can get 100 miles per gallon and a 40% power increase. So, this means if you have a 200-horsepower car, just by switching to water you will get an extra 80 horsepower increase. Talk about high performance! This fuel is called HHO and there are a couple ways to make it from water. One way can be electrolysis, or another way is with sound. The electrolysis is definably the easiest, but also the least efficient.

Another way to beat high fuel prices are with an electric car. Now I am not talking about your normal electric car that runs on batteries. That's crazy. Why would you want something you will need recharging every night? What I am talking about is the type of electric car Nikola Tesla had in the 1930's. Have you ever heard about Nikola Tesla? He is the real inventor of electricity. He discovered Alternative Current in the 1890's. This is the electricity we all use today, but for some reason there is very little mentioned of him in our history books. Thomas Edison only discovered Direct Current. This is type found in a battery. Tesla's electric car was a Piece Arrow. He used a normal electric motor that was powered by his Oscillator Shuttle circuit. This circuit would power the electric motor with all the energy it would ever need. His car was reported to run up to 80 miles per hour, ran whisper quiet, and NEVER needs refueling.

Final Words

I've shown you we have the technology to make energy for free, you can get it from water to rotating shafts to magnets to even crystals. All these machines are somehow making a simple dipole that is extracting free energy right out of the environment. A simple dipole can be a battery, the terminals of a generator, any two-pole magnet like a bar magnet, and atom with a positive and negative charge, the earth's magnetic field, the sun, or even another Galaxy. Currently electrical systems deliberately only use their current once and do not replenish it from the active environment. All electrical circuits have been deliberately forced into being equal with the active environment around it. With this set up, circuits are made to consume the energy instead of replenishing it. It's too bad considering if the circle is tuned to be out of balance it would make more energy than we could ever use. Let me give you this one last example to help you better understand what is happening here. Let's take a regular item like a TV remote, it runs on batteries most people would say that this remote is powered by the batteries, but this is not true. What is really happening here is the battery is making a simple dipole. The dipole is pulling energy in from the environment around it to power the remote. Since this circuit is set up to be in balance with the active environment it will quickly drain the battery. When the battery runs out of chemical energy to make the dipole, the power is gone and the remote will not work. Now if we set up the circuit in the TV remote to be out of balance with the active environment around it, the remote will pull in energy to power it. Then if we take a little power the same amount as it takes to make the dipole and send it back to the battery this TV remote will run until the battery won't hold a charge anymore. This could be up to 40 years' time. The truth is there is tons of energy all around us to use we were literally floating in a vast sea of free energy. The choice really comes down to whether we use it. The only reason we are currently using the same old expensive and wasteful sources is purely greed and the giant energy companies make 440 billion dollars a year off us for what we could get for practically nothing. Just think about it for a minute, how much do you spend a month on energy, you know things like gasoline gas to heat your home and electricity to run all your stuff. $200 a month? $400 a month? $600 a month? Imagine having that extra money in your pocket? Well $400 a month in savings adds up to almost $5000.00 a year.

In conclusion, if you found this book helpful in learning more about renewable energy principles, please be sure to leave a positive review on Amazon.com, America's largest e-marketplace and bookstore. For more information visit Sustainability.Energy or EnergyBook.info.